JFK'$ Coincidental Death Note Discovery

By

Ernest H. Green

authorHOUSE™

1663 LIBERTY DRIVE, SUITE 200
BLOOMINGTON, INDIANA 47403
(800) 839-8640
WWW.AUTHORHOUSE.COM

First published by AuthorHouse 03/31/05

ISBN: 1-4208-1032-4 (sc)

Printed in the United States of America
Bloomington, Indiana

This book is printed on acid-free paper.

DISCOVERY OF THIS STARTLING

EVENT WAS UNVEILED ON

MEMORIAL DAY WEEKEND 1965

The author of this story is of

no prime importance, only and

only the information that you

read will this you find.

PREFACE

This entire story is indeed $trange—but true and by a mere coincident unveiled right before the eyes of million$ the world over.

However, *we should never forget* that always and forever there will be a very first event of *WORLD* importance to become known for a very *first* time.

I speak of our late President "John F. Kennedy" and the certain one dollar bill. Now this factual story might suggest that he was, beyond a doubt, the greatest commander-in-chief of our time. This is your opinion, to have, and to hold. Whatever your mind thinks, and believes, then that becomes the way it really is to you. Good, bad, indifferent, or otherwise. To the million$ of readers wherever you may be please evaluate your own mind as you proceed to read this once in a lifetime startling story, and also try to remember that nothing in life is ever complete, including this story of JFK and the one ($1.00) dollar bill.

INTRODUCTION

Time and money are here to stay. Both were before our time and is an undisputed fact that it will remain after our time. Life, too, was here before our time, and also will be forever. However, we are only concerned of course with our very own. And only our maker (God) knows when it (life) will end.

JFK, was a very exceptional President of all time, and yet, there have been others, there will be more. But first he was a man. Common things, how common is a one dollar bill? Very common to million$ of people the world over. People earn and spend the dollar out of *necessity* and for many other reasons. Most of the things we do in life stem from force of habit and value too often is misplaced and always will be. What you have read to this point is nothing that you have not heard or read before. And so in life it is said that nothing is new. It is only different when learned of by one for a first time.

So very much has been said of and about JFK and his life. Yet man, himself, cannot ascertain his own greatness. Man is motivated by something or someone, he does nothing for no one without doing something for himself. Do we, or don't we know that for every cause there is truly an effect.

Most things in life hinge upon what the one dollar ($1.00) will or will not do. Whether JFK's Death Note is coincidental or factual is found on the $1.00 dollar bill. No place in history has it been found that a President's Death Note is, for all to see, printed or minted on legal tender of U. S. currency. From the Father of Our Country, George Washington (whose picture appears on the one dollar bill) to the late fallen warrior, JFK, is history and indeed historical.

There are 12 Federal *Reserve* Banks in the United States. Atlanta, Georgia; San Francisco, Calif.; Minneapolis, Minn.; Richmond, Virginia; Kansas City, Mo.; Philadelphia, Pa.; Boston, Mass.; Cleveland, Ohio; New York, N.Y.; and Chicago, Ill. Dallas, Texas is the 11th one. This city and state is our concern.

There were thirty-four Presidents before JFK was elected to office. ("Their names are of no importance and not relative to this story.) The fact remains that his greatness is now and has been discovered on a certain one ($1.00) dollar bill. Now nothing becomes a first until proven and established. There have been many claims for a *first,* there will be more.

We know the dollar bill and accept it for what it is worth as all other things. The one ($1.00) bill is legal tender for all debts public and private. JFK has paid all debts public and private and our debt is yet to be paid. We come into life in debt and we die in debt. We do hold the most prized possession of it all — life, coupled with good health. Whatever else that money will buy other than food, clothing, and shelter and other necessities becomes secondary.

Success is only measured in terms of dollars. Have you ever seen a man proclaim to be just that without it? Yet we know of no dollaraires, only the millionaire. Though, one must have the $1.00 first.

Money, man robs, steals and even will and has killed for the one dollar bill and even less. Money means different things to different people. However, it will do but so much and no more. Never a day passes in our lives, since we first became acquainted with money, that we don't think about it, or talk about it, or earn it. More effort goes into man for making money than anything else.

The one dollar bill is and will be called many things. The legal name is what is printed or minted on the face and backside. They read The United States of America. This Note is Legal Tender for All Debts, Public and Private. Washington, D.C. Then the numbers, initials, signatures. On the reverse side the message *In God We Trust.*

Coin collectors advertise for certain coins because a certain value has been placed on them. Everyone at one time or another has borrowed or has loaned money—from the very poor to the very rich. The million$ of readers who are reading this story or who have so done, have given money to, or for something. Do we give money for something? There can be but one answer yes. It is only said once again. No one has ever done anything for gratis.

Few people will admit to these facts. So simply ask yourself, have you?

JFK was only as great as he was acclaimed by the people of his country. The greatness of our beloved President speaks for itself—through every media of news. And now, his strength and power is found on a one dollar bill. Any other denomination that may be found does not have the significance and neither would it have the meaning. This is a once in a lifetime, strange, startling, fictional, and coincidental story, but true!

JFK's DEATH NOTE

John F. Kennedy was our 35th President and the first Roman Catholic of our time. Bold and young, warm and fearless. Mr. Kennedy was also the youngest *chief* of our time. He was many things to many people. Mere words fall too short in trying to describe a man oh so great.

George Washington, was the Father of our Country. His picture compliments the one ($1.00) dollar bill and it will forever remain until an act of Congress replaces it.

Our late chief, JFK, or the White House was informed (as it has been said) that it was unsafe to continue or to begin the planned tour in Texas. However, the warning (if true) was not heeded. Thus a chapter and history was recorded. There were six (6) tours, or speeches to be made or both, tours and speeches. San Antonio, Austin, Dallas, Houston, Fort Worth and (not necessarily in that order). It was in "Big D" as it is known to many when his fatal motorcade came to an untimely end. To million$ of Americans, to this day, have never looked at and analyzed the certain Death Note of JFK on the one dollar bill.

People by nature simply find it very difficult to accept a first for the very first time. The mind of man subconsciously rejects this fact.

On the face of this particular one dollar bill is the letter (K) encircled within these words which read Federal Reserve Bank of Dallas, Texas. That (K) is for Kennedy.

The (K) means much more than any other letter on a one dollar bill. We now know that Dallas, Texas will long be in the minds of Americans, if not the world. Simple mention of Dallas, and dear reader, what are you to think of then? Our 35th President was in Dallas, Texas and that our country had lost forever a *truly great leader.* Gone but not forgotten but forever remembered. Shocked and stunned as we were but *life waits for no man big or small.* Will we ever forget those four (4) dark days? From all four (4) corners of the world came the greatest leaders to pay their final tribute to a man that the world shall never, never forget. The Duke, the Duchess, the Kings and the Queens and other dignitaries of the highest order.

Every famous man is remembered by many things that he might have said or done. We tend to remember, many things that a man may say. "I Shall Return," upon hearing such a quote, we think of but one man. We World War Two veterans will know to be sure. General Douglas MacAuthur

"Give Me Liberty or Give Me Death,"

Patrick Henry 3-23-1775 by those who have made their niche in history. This writer, and author is not remotely attempting to make them all. This task would become dubious and quite arduous.

"Ask Not What Your Country Can Do For You, But Ask What You Can Do For Your Country." Such depth with greater meaning. Those 18 words spoken by Mr. Kennedy were lived by our chief. When the lyrich are sung, *This Is My Country!* We may well remember JFK. Oh, say can you see on this one ($1.00) dollar bill that I have explained to you, the number eleven appears 4 times.

JFK was in Dallas, Texas in the month of November. The 11th month in the year is just that. Now, what we know is one thing, and what we think is something else or, "It is better to know a little than to think a lot." Quote.

It was fate and just a coincident for our late young, handsome, dynamic President to meet with his Maker or Master, in the very same home state as the then Vice President, who is now the President of the United States, LBJ,

Kennedy's, one ($1.00) dollar bill, as of this writing, is but a dollar. In time, his "Death Note" will become hard to find, and a rare piece of currency. You can be positively sure, that once this amazing truth has been learned. And also considering the fact that JFK served his country *without* a salary.

Anything of value, that we ever hope to have, is not the price high? Or don't we spend the time, energy, and effort to have whatever? So now, I ask you dear reader, what will you pay at this very moment to have peace of mind?

In God We Trust. This message you will find on the one ($1.00) dollar bill. (This writer knows this too well since the larger bills are rare to his hands.) That is what JFK did when he commenced his tour on the fatal morning of November 22, 1963. The warnings meant nothing (if there were any) bold, daring, and forever understanding, his duty to his country came first. Words fail again to describe one so great. JFK knew, that time is only *borrowed* and *time waits for no man, man waits for time.*

Be it well, to always remember, that when death comes, our work here on earth is finished. Life goes on — whatever you may have done in this world, big or small, someone you might not know has been helped. We do know that JFK did so very much and for so many, is now yet giving— giving his memories that we all share. We have so much to be thankful for.

Life is the most precious thing that we have and should be treated as such. Everything could never be said about our late Commander in Chief, However, look at the next $1.00 bill that you have or will receive. It could be.... JFK'$

DEATH NOTE

Summary of the $ 1.00 bill.

The Dollar bill that is the essence of this note is the "K" series. The "11" on the four corners represent the District. Having said there are 12 Federal Reserve, Banks, Coincidental as it is, November is the 11 Month of the year 1963 is the year that this particular $1.00 was in circulation.

Our 35th President John F. Kennedy was in Dallas Texas. The Federal Reserved District for Dallas is K-11 Thus, In the month of November 1963, J.F.K. made his transition by means of assassination.

$$$$$$$$$$$$$$$$

Understanding the Design and Symbolism of the U.S. One Dollar Bill

Although symbols are open to many interpretations, I believe the following information offers some historical insight (and some undocumented perceptions) about the design and meaning of some of the images on the one dollar bill. The explanations and interpretations that appear below were verified by the Truth or Fiction website, and predominantly (except where noted otherwise) reflect the official interpretations of the United States Treasury Department and the United States Department of State, the official keeper of the United States Seal.

Take out a dollar bill and study it.

The one dollar bill you're looking at first came off the presses in 1957 in its present design. According to the U.S.

Treasury Department, that is when the motto "In God We Trust" started being used on paper money. It was in use on coins long before that.

This so-called paper money is in fact a cotton and linen blend, with red and blue minute silk fibers running through it. It is actually material. We've all washed it without it falling apart. A special blend of ink is used, the contents we will never know. It is overprinted with symbols and then it is starched to make it water resistant and pressed to give it that nice crisp look.

If you look on the front of the bill, you will see the United States Treasury Seal. Although some claims have been made that the scales represent the need for a balanced budget, the Treasury Department has little to do with whether the budget is balanced, since that is actually handled by congress. The U.S. Treasury Department indicates that the balancing scales actually represent justice. In the center, some people believe there is a carpenter's T-square, a tool used for an even cut. But that image is actually a chevron with 13 stars representing the 13 original colonies. Underneath is a key that is intended to represent a symbol of authority.

If you turn the bill over, you will see two circles. The two circles reflect the two sides of the Great Seal of the United

States. Before the adjournment of the Continental Congress on July 4th, 1776, a committee was appointed to develop a seal for the United States. The committee was Benjamin Franklin, John Adams, and Thomas Jefferson, three of the five men who had drafted the Declaration of Independence. They were merely the first committee, however. It took six years, the work of two additional committees and a total of 14 men before a final version of the Great Seal was approved. The final proposal, as accepted by Congress, was submitted on June 13,1782, by Charles Thompson, Secretary of Congress. He brought together some of the recommendations of the three committees, their consultants, and artists.

If you look at the left hand circle, you will see a Pyramid. This pyramid was not a part of the proposals for the Great Seal unit the third committee, and it was not suggested by Jefferson, Franklin, and Adams. Notice the face is lighted and the western side is dark. Although there is no "official" explanation for the shading, some interpret it as a reflection that our country was just beginning and had not begun to explore the West or decided what we could do for Western Civilization.

The Pyramid is UN-capped, which may signify that our country was not yet unfinished. The unfinished state of the pyramid was intentional, and Charles Thompson, in his remarks to congress about the symbolism on the Great Seal, said the pyramid represented "Strength and Duration." Inside the capstone you have the all-seeing eye, an ancient symbol for divinity. Although Franklin's committee did not suggest a pyramid, it did originate the suggestion of the eye. However, the term "all-seeing eye" was never officially used when describing it. The Franklin committee wanted the seal to include a reflection of divine providence and discussed a variety of themes including the Children of Israel in the Wilderness.

"IN GOD WE TRUST" is on this currency. The Latin above the pyramid, ANNUIT COEPTIS, means "God has favored our undertaking." It was Franklin's belief that one man couldn't do it alone, but a group of men with the help of God could do anything. The Latin below the pyramid, NOVUS ORDO SECLORUM, is interpreted to mean "a new order for the world." At the base of the pyramid is the Roman Numeral for 1776.

If you look at the right-hand circle, and check it carefully, you may notice that with only slight modifications it is the Seal of the President of the United States. It also appears on every National Cemetery in the United States, the Parade of Flags Walkway at the Bushnell, Florida National Cemetery, and is the centerpiece of most heroes' monuments. On the Great Seal, the eagle faces the talon holding the olive branch. The eagle on The Presidential Seal faced in the opposite direction-toward the talon holding the arrows until 1945, when Harry Truman had it redesigned to face the olive branch as well.

No one knows for certain what the symbols mean. But although there is no explanation of the imagery of the eagle in the official records, most historical references to the bald eagle indicate that it represents something of uniquely American origin. One of the original design proposals for the Great Seal featured a small crested white eagle, which is not uniquely American, but this was later changed to the uniquely American Bald Eagle. An unsupported interpretation of the inclusion of the Bald Eagle is that it could also represent victory and independence, because the eagle is not afraid of a storm, is strong and smart enough to soar above it, and wears no material crown.

Also, notice the shield is unsupported. Charles Thompson said it denoted that the United States of America ought to rely on their own virtue. The shield consists of red and white stripes with a blue bar above that represents Congress. The colors are taken from the American flag and officially the red represents hardiness and valor, the white represents purity and innocence, and the blue, vigilance, perseverance, and justice. In the Eagle's beak you will read, "E PLURIBUS UNUN", meaning "<u>one nation for many people.</u>"

Above the Eagle you have thirteen stars representing the thirteen original colonies. Again, we were coming together as one. Notice that the Eagle holds an olive branch and arrows in his talons. The official meaning is that the olive branch and the arrows "denote the power of peace and war." As noted previously, the design shows the eagle facing the olive branch. This was the opposite of the Presidential Seal, which showed the eagle facing the arrows, until President Harry Truman had it redesigned to face the olive branch in 1945."

Some feel that the number 13 is an unlucky number. You will usually never see a room numbered 13, or hotels or motels with a 13th floor. But the significance of the number 13 in U.S. history is very strong. The number 13 as used on many U.S. symbols (the stripes on the flag, steps on the Pyramid, 13 stars above the eagle, 13 plumes of feathers on each of the Eagle's wings, 13 bars on the shield, 13 leaves on the olive branch, 13 fruits, and 13 arrows) all represent the beginning of our country, as established by the thirteen colonies. But it should also remind us of the importance of the "13th Amendment". And you can, and should, be reminded of the history of this country each time you look at a one dollar bill.

Visit the Museum of Currency, San Francisco, CA.

NOTES

NOTES

NOTES

NOTES

NOTES

NOTES

NOTES

NOTES

NOTES

NOTES

NOTES

NOTES

NOTES

NOTES

NOTES

NOTES

NOTES

NOTES

NOTES

NOTES

NOTES

NOTES